Anxiety Journal

FOR CHILDREN

BY KELLY DAY

DISCLAIMER:
I am not a counsellor, Doctor or mental health professional. I
created this journal because the contents work for my child
right now and I thought others may find it useful.

If you believe your child may be facing any kind of mental
health crisis, I would strongly encourage you to contact a
registered medical professional in your country and follow
their advice.

What is Anxiety?

Anxiety is something that we all (grownups and kids) have at times. Sometimes it will feel like fear or worry, but sometimes it can also make you feel upset and angry, other times it can make you feel physically unwell. Anxiety can be really tricky, because it doesn't always look like panic or fear, sometimes it can mean that you have trouble sleeping or lead to physical sensations like fatigue (tiredness), headaches, or stomach aches.

Often, our very clever brains can work through our anxiety, and it simply goes away; but sometimes it hangs around, even when we don't want it to. If that is happening to you right now, you will know that it's not much fun. In fact, it can make you feel overwhelmed, sad, tired and it can feel pretty lonely. Just know that you're not alone; a lot of children are going through the same thing right now. In fact, I happen to know one of those children very well, – we'll call her 'Miss A' and she is the reason this book was created!

As we are growing up, we sometimes worry about things that we think grownups, or friends, will think are strange, or funny – so we don't share those worries with them. The problem is, when we don't share our worries, they can grow and become so overwhelming that it seems like we will never get past them. That is where this journal comes in.

On the days that you are anxious/worried/scared or upset, this book is here to help you (and your grownups) work through how you are feeling. If you share your journal with your grownups, it also becomes a good way of letting your grownups know what is happening in your head. I know 'Miss A' finds writing her worries down and leaving it for me each night (like a 'worry message book') really helps her as it means we can talk about those worries together and help ease her anxiety. We are working towards beating her anxiety, and I hope with the help of your grownups, you can do that too.

Kelly xxx

Date: ....

Today my anxiety level is: Low | Medium | High

I think that my anxiety today has been triggered by:

I plan to manage my anxiety today by using:

☐ Deep breathing

☐ Meditation

☐ Exercise

☐ Grounding *(3 things)*

☐ Aromatherapy

☐ Talk Therapy

Three things I am proud of myself for today:

1)

2)

3)

Something that calmed me down today was:

What I would like to say to my 'Anxious Self' today:

This is what I would like my grown up's to know today:

HEALTHY BODY: HEALTHY MIND

Helping my body stay healthy, also helps my mind:

Today I supported my body & mind by staying hydrated:

Water: Colour in the water bottles as you finish them

Getting enough sleep helps my brain face the day:

Tonight I will go to bed at: ____ pm

Date: ....

Today my anxiety level is: Low | Medium | High

I think that my anxiety today has been triggered by:

I plan to manage my anxiety today by using:

☐ Deep breathing   ☐ Grounding *(3 things)*

☐ Meditation   ☐ Aromatherapy

☐ Exercise   ☐ Talk Therapy

Three things I am proud of myself for today:

1)

2)

3)

Something that calmed me down today was:

What I would like to say to my 'Anxious Self' today:

This is what I would like my grown up's to know today:

HEALTHY BODY: HEALTHY MIND

Helping my body stay healthy, also helps my mind:

Today I supported my body & mind by staying hydrated:

Water: Colour in the water bottles as you finish them

Getting enough sleep helps my brain face the day:

Tonight I will go to bed at: ____ pm

Date: ....

Today my anxiety level is: Low | Medium | High

I think that my anxiety today has been triggered by:

I plan to manage my anxiety today by using:

☐	Deep breathing	☐	Grounding *(3 things)*
☐	Meditation	☐	Aromatherapy
☐	Exercise	☐	Talk Therapy

Three things I am proud of myself for today:

1)

2)

3)

Something that calmed me down today was:

What I would like to say to my 'Anxious Self' today:

This is what I would like my grown up's to know today:

HEALTHY BODY: HEALTHY MIND

Helping my body stay healthy, also helps my mind:

Today I supported my body & mind by staying hydrated:

Water: Colour in the water bottles as you finish them

Getting enough sleep helps my brain face the day:

Tonight I will go to bed at: ___ pm

Date: ....

Today my anxiety level is: Low | Medium | High

I think that my anxiety today has been triggered by:

I plan to manage my anxiety today by using:

☐ Deep breathing   ☐ Grounding *(3 things)*

☐ Meditation   ☐ Aromatherapy

☐ Exercise   ☐ Talk Therapy

Three things I am proud of myself for today:

1)

2)

3)

Something that calmed me down today was:

What I would like to say to my 'Anxious Self' today:

This is what I would like my grown up's to know today:

HEALTHY BODY: HEALTHY MIND

Helping my body stay healthy, also helps my mind:

Today I supported my body & mind by staying hydrated:

Water: Colour in the water bottles as you finish them

Getting enough sleep helps my brain face the day:

Tonight I will go to bed at: ___ pm

Date: ....

Today my anxiety level is: Low | Medium | High

I think that my anxiety today has been triggered by:

I plan to manage my anxiety today by using:

☐ Deep breathing   ☐ Grounding *(3 things)*

☐ Meditation   ☐ Aromatherapy

☐ Exercise   ☐ Talk Therapy

Three things I am proud of myself for today:

1)

2)

3)

Something that calmed me down today was:

What I would like to say to my 'Anxious Self' today:

This is what I would like my grown up's to know today:

HEALTHY BODY: HEALTHY MIND

Helping my body stay healthy, also helps my mind:

Today I supported my body & mind by staying hydrated:

Water: Colour in the water bottles as you finish them

Getting enough sleep helps my brain face the day:

Tonight I will go to bed at: ____ pm

Date: ....

Today my anxiety level is: Low | Medium | High

I think that my anxiety today has been triggered by:

I plan to manage my anxiety today by using:

☐ Deep breathing   ☐ Grounding *(3 things)*

☐ Meditation   ☐ Aromatherapy

☐ Exercise   ☐ Talk Therapy

Three things I am proud of myself for today:

1)

2)

3)

Something that calmed me down today was:

What I would like to say to my 'Anxious Self' today:

This is what I would like my grown up's to know today:

HEALTHY BODY: HEALTHY MIND

Helping my body stay healthy, also helps my mind:

Today I supported my body & mind by staying hydrated:

Water: Colour in the water bottles as you finish them

Getting enough sleep helps my brain face the day:

Tonight I will go to bed at: ____ pm

Date: ....

Today my anxiety level is: Low | Medium | High

I think that my anxiety today has been triggered by:

I plan to manage my anxiety today by using:

☐ Deep breathing   ☐ Grounding *(3 things)*

☐ Meditation   ☐ Aromatherapy

☐ Exercise   ☐ Talk Therapy

Three things I am proud of myself for today:

1)

2)

3)

Something that calmed me down today was:

What I would like to say to my 'Anxious Self' today:

This is what I would like my grown up's to know today:

HEALTHY BODY: HEALTHY MIND

Helping my body stay healthy, also helps my mind:

Today I supported my body & mind by staying hydrated:

Water: Colour in the water bottles as you finish them

Getting enough sleep helps my brain face the day:

Tonight I will go to bed at: ____ pm

Date: ....

Today my anxiety level is: Low | Medium | High

I think that my anxiety today has been triggered by:

I plan to manage my anxiety today by using:

☐ Deep breathing   ☐ Grounding *(3 things)*

☐ Meditation   ☐ Aromatherapy

☐ Exercise   ☐ Talk Therapy

Three things I am proud of myself for today:

1)

2)

3)

Something that calmed me down today was:

What I would like to say to my 'Anxious Self' today:

This is what I would like my grown up's to know today:

HEALTHY BODY: HEALTHY MIND

Helping my body stay healthy, also helps my mind:

Today I supported my body & mind by staying hydrated:

Water: Colour in the water bottles as you finish them

Getting enough sleep helps my brain face the day:

Tonight I will go to bed at: ____ pm

Date: ....

Today my anxiety level is: Low | Medium | High

I think that my anxiety today has been triggered by:

I plan to manage my anxiety today by using:

☐ Deep breathing   ☐ Grounding *(3 things)*

☐ Meditation   ☐ Aromatherapy

☐ Exercise   ☐ Talk Therapy

Three things I am proud of myself for today:

1)

2)

3)

Something that calmed me down today was:

What I would like to say to my 'Anxious Self' today:

This is what I would like my grown up's to know today:

HEALTHY BODY: HEALTHY MIND

Helping my body stay healthy, also helps my mind:

Today I supported my body & mind by staying hydrated:

Water: ⛶ ⛶ ⛶ ⛶ ⛶ Colour in the water bottles as you finish them

Getting enough sleep helps my brain face the day:

Tonight I will go to bed at: ___ pm

Date: ....

Today my anxiety level is: Low | Medium | High

I think that my anxiety today has been triggered by:

I plan to manage my anxiety today by using:

☐ Deep breathing   ☐ Grounding *(3 things)*

☐ Meditation   ☐ Aromatherapy

☐ Exercise   ☐ Talk Therapy

Three things I am proud of myself for today:

1)

2)

3)

Something that calmed me down today was:

What I would like to say to my 'Anxious Self' today:

This is what I would like my grown up's to know today:

HEALTHY BODY: HEALTHY MIND

Helping my body stay healthy, also helps my mind:

Today I supported my body & mind by staying hydrated:

Water: Colour in the water bottles as you finish them

Getting enough sleep helps my brain face the day:

Tonight I will go to bed at: ____ pm

Date: ....

Today my anxiety level is: Low | Medium | High

I think that my anxiety today has been triggered by:

I plan to manage my anxiety today by using:

☐ Deep breathing   ☐ Grounding *(3 things)*

☐ Meditation   ☐ Aromatherapy

☐ Exercise   ☐ Talk Therapy

Three things I am proud of myself for today:

1)

2)

3)

Something that calmed me down today was:

What I would like to say to my 'Anxious Self' today:

This is what I would like my grown up's to know today:

HEALTHY BODY: HEALTHY MIND

Helping my body stay healthy, also helps my mind:

Today I supported my body & mind by staying hydrated:

Water: Colour in the water bottles as you finish them

Getting enough sleep helps my brain face the day:

Tonight I will go to bed at: ____ pm

Date: ....

Today my anxiety level is: Low | Medium | High

I think that my anxiety today has been triggered by:

I plan to manage my anxiety today by using:

☐ Deep breathing   ☐ Grounding *(3 things)*

☐ Meditation   ☐ Aromatherapy

☐ Exercise   ☐ Talk Therapy

Three things I am proud of myself for today:

1)

2)

3)

Something that calmed me down today was:

What I would like to say to my 'Anxious Self' today:

This is what I would like my grown up's to know today:

HEALTHY BODY: HEALTHY MIND

Helping my body stay healthy, also helps my mind:

Today I supported my body & mind by staying hydrated:

Water: Colour in the water bottles as you finish them

Getting enough sleep helps my brain face the day:

Tonight I will go to bed at: ____ pm

Date:

Today my anxiety level is: Low | Medium | High

I think that my anxiety today has been triggered by:

I plan to manage my anxiety today by using:

☐ Deep breathing   ☐ Grounding *(3 things)*

☐ Meditation   ☐ Aromatherapy

☐ Exercise   ☐ Talk Therapy

Three things I am proud of myself for today:

1)

2)

3)

Something that calmed me down today was:

What I would like to say to my 'Anxious Self' today:

This is what I would like my grown up's to know today:

HEALTHY BODY: HEALTHY MIND

Helping my body stay healthy, also helps my mind:

Today I supported my body & mind by staying hydrated:

Water: Colour in the water bottles as you finish them

Getting enough sleep helps my brain face the day:

Tonight I will go to bed at: ____ pm

Date: ....

Today my anxiety level is: Low | Medium | High

I think that my anxiety today has been triggered by:

I plan to manage my anxiety today by using:

☐   Deep breathing   ☐   Grounding *(3 things)*

☐   Meditation   ☐   Aromatherapy

☐   Exercise   ☐   Talk Therapy

Three things I am proud of myself for today:

1)

2)

3)

Something that calmed me down today was:

What I would like to say to my 'Anxious Self' today:

This is what I would like my grown up's to know today:

HEALTHY BODY: HEALTHY MIND

Helping my body stay healthy, also helps my mind:

Today I supported my body & mind by staying hydrated:

Water: Colour in the water bottles as you finish them

Getting enough sleep helps my brain face the day:

Tonight I will go to bed at: ____ pm

Date: ....

Today my anxiety level is: Low | Medium | High

I think that my anxiety today has been triggered by:

I plan to manage my anxiety today by using:

☐ Deep breathing ☐ Grounding *(3 things)*

☐ Meditation ☐ Aromatherapy

☐ Exercise ☐ Talk Therapy

Three things I am proud of myself for today:

1)

2)

3)

Something that calmed me down today was:

What I would like to say to my 'Anxious Self' today:

This is what I would like my grown up's to know today:

HEALTHY BODY: HEALTHY MIND

Helping my body stay healthy, also helps my mind:

Today I supported my body & mind by staying hydrated:

Water: Colour in the water bottles as you finish them

Getting enough sleep helps my brain face the day:

Tonight I will go to bed at: ___ pm

Date: ....

Today my anxiety level is: Low | Medium | High

I think that my anxiety today has been triggered by:

I plan to manage my anxiety today by using:

☐ Deep breathing   ☐ Grounding *(3 things)*

☐ Meditation   ☐ Aromatherapy

☐ Exercise   ☐ Talk Therapy

Three things I am proud of myself for today:

1)

2)

3)

Something that calmed me down today was:

What I would like to say to my 'Anxious Self' today:

This is what I would like my grown up's to know today:

HEALTHY BODY: HEALTHY MIND

Helping my body stay healthy, also helps my mind:

Today I supported my body & mind by staying hydrated:

Water: Colour in the water bottles as you finish them

Getting enough sleep helps my brain face the day:

Tonight I will go to bed at: ____ pm

Date: ....

Today my anxiety level is: Low | Medium | High

I think that my anxiety today has been triggered by:

I plan to manage my anxiety today by using:

☐ Deep breathing   ☐ Grounding *(3 things)*

☐ Meditation   ☐ Aromatherapy

☐ Exercise   ☐ Talk Therapy

Three things I am proud of myself for today:

1)

2)

3)

Something that calmed me down today was:

What I would like to say to my 'Anxious Self' today:

This is what I would like my grown up's to know today:

HEALTHY BODY: HEALTHY MIND

Helping my body stay healthy, also helps my mind:

Today I supported my body & mind by staying hydrated:

Water: Colour in the water bottles as you finish them

Getting enough sleep helps my brain face the day:

Tonight I will go to bed at: _____ pm

Date: ....

Today my anxiety level is: Low | Medium | High

I think that my anxiety today has been triggered by:

I plan to manage my anxiety today by using:

☐ Deep breathing   ☐ Grounding *(3 things)*

☐ Meditation   ☐ Aromatherapy

☐ Exercise   ☐ Talk Therapy

Three things I am proud of myself for today:

1)

2)

3)

Something that calmed me down today was:

What I would like to say to my 'Anxious Self' today:

This is what I would like my grown up's to know today:

Helping my body stay healthy, also helps my mind:

Today I supported my body & mind by staying hydrated:

Water: Colour in the water bottles as you finish them

Getting enough sleep helps my brain face the day:

Tonight I will go to bed at: ____ pm

Date: ....

Today my anxiety level is: Low | Medium | High

I think that my anxiety today has been triggered by:

I plan to manage my anxiety today by using:

☐ Deep breathing   ☐ Grounding *(3 things)*

☐ Meditation   ☐ Aromatherapy

☐ Exercise   ☐ Talk Therapy

Three things I am proud of myself for today:

1)

2)

3)

Something that calmed me down today was:

What I would like to say to my 'Anxious Self' today:

This is what I would like my grown up's to know today:

HEALTHY BODY: HEALTHY MIND

Helping my body stay healthy, also helps my mind:

Today I supported my body & mind by staying hydrated:

Water: 🍼 🍼 🍼 🍼 🍼 Colour in the water bottles as you finish them

Getting enough sleep helps my brain face the day:

Tonight I will go to bed at: ___ pm

Date: ....

Today my anxiety level is: Low | Medium | High

I think that my anxiety today has been triggered by:

I plan to manage my anxiety today by using:

☐ Deep breathing   ☐ Grounding *(3 things)*

☐ Meditation   ☐ Aromatherapy

☐ Exercise   ☐ Talk Therapy

Three things I am proud of myself for today:

1)

2)

3)

Something that calmed me down today was:

What I would like to say to my 'Anxious Self' today:

This is what I would like my grown up's to know today:

HEALTHY BODY: HEALTHY MIND

Helping my body stay healthy, also helps my mind:

Today I supported my body & mind by staying hydrated:

Water: 〇〇〇〇〇 Colour in the water bottles as you finish them

Getting enough sleep helps my brain face the day:

Tonight I will go to bed at: ___ pm

Date: ....

Today my anxiety level is: Low | Medium | High

I think that my anxiety today has been triggered by:

I plan to manage my anxiety today by using:

☐ Deep breathing   ☐ Grounding (3 things)

☐ Meditation   ☐ Aromatherapy

☐ Exercise   ☐ Talk Therapy

Three things I am proud of myself for today:

1)

2)

3)

Something that calmed me down today was:

What I would like to say to my 'Anxious Self' today:

This is what I would like my grown up's to know today:

HEALTHY BODY: HEALTHY MIND

Helping my body stay healthy, also helps my mind:

Today I supported my body & mind by staying hydrated:

Water: Colour in the water bottles as you finish them

Getting enough sleep helps my brain face the day:

Tonight I will go to bed at: ____ pm

Date: ....

Today my anxiety level is: Low | Medium | High

I think that my anxiety today has been triggered by:

I plan to manage my anxiety today by using:

☐ Deep breathing   ☐ Grounding *(3 things)*

☐ Meditation   ☐ Aromatherapy

☐ Exercise   ☐ Talk Therapy

Three things I am proud of myself for today:

1)

2)

3)

Something that calmed me down today was:

What I would like to say to my 'Anxious Self' today:

This is what I would like my grown up's to know today:

HEALTHY BODY: HEALTHY MIND

Helping my body stay healthy, also helps my mind:

Today I supported my body & mind by staying hydrated:

Water: Colour in the water bottles as you finish them

Getting enough sleep helps my brain face the day:

Tonight I will go to bed at: ___ pm

Date: ....

Today my anxiety level is: Low | Medium | High

I think that my anxiety today has been triggered by:

I plan to manage my anxiety today by using:

☐ Deep breathing   ☐ Grounding *(3 things)*

☐ Meditation   ☐ Aromatherapy

☐ Exercise   ☐ Talk Therapy

Three things I am proud of myself for today:

1)

2)

3)

Something that calmed me down today was:

What I would like to say to my 'Anxious Self' today:

This is what I would like my grown up's to know today:

HEALTHY BODY: HEALTHY MIND

Helping my body stay healthy, also helps my mind:

Today I supported my body & mind by staying hydrated:

Water: Colour in the water bottles as you finish them

Getting enough sleep helps my brain face the day:

Tonight I will go to bed at: ____ pm

Date:

Today my anxiety level is: Low | Medium | High

I think that my anxiety today has been triggered by:

I plan to manage my anxiety today by using:

☐ Deep breathing   ☐ Grounding *(3 things)*

☐ Meditation   ☐ Aromatherapy

☐ Exercise   ☐ Talk Therapy

Three things I am proud of myself for today:

1)

2)

3)

Something that calmed me down today was:

What I would like to say to my 'Anxious Self' today:

This is what I would like my grown up's to know today:

HEALTHY BODY: HEALTHY MIND

Helping my body stay healthy, also helps my mind:

Today I supported my body & mind by staying hydrated:

Water: Colour in the water bottles as you finish them

Getting enough sleep helps my brain face the day:

Tonight I will go to bed at: ____ pm

Date: _____

Today my anxiety level is: Low | Medium | High

I think that my anxiety today has been triggered by:

I plan to manage my anxiety today by using:

☐ Deep breathing   ☐ Grounding *(3 things)*

☐ Meditation   ☐ Aromatherapy

☐ Exercise   ☐ Talk Therapy

Three things I am proud of myself for today:

1)

2)

3)

Something that calmed me down today was:

What I would like to say to my 'Anxious Self' today:

This is what I would like my grown up's to know today:

HEALTHY BODY: HEALTHY MIND

Helping my body stay healthy, also helps my mind:

Today I supported my body & mind by staying hydrated:

Water: ⛶ ⛶ ⛶ ⛶ ⛶   Colour in the water bottles as you finish them

Getting enough sleep helps my brain face the day:

Tonight I will go to bed at: ____ pm

Date: ....

Today my anxiety level is: Low | Medium | High

I think that my anxiety today has been triggered by:

I plan to manage my anxiety today by using:

☐   Deep breathing   ☐   Grounding *(3 things)*

☐   Meditation   ☐   Aromatherapy

☐   Exercise   ☐   Talk Therapy

Three things I am proud of myself for today:

1)

2)

3)

Something that calmed me down today was:

What I would like to say to my 'Anxious Self' today:

This is what I would like my grown up's to know today:

HEALTHY BODY: HEALTHY MIND

Helping my body stay healthy, also helps my mind:

Today I supported my body & mind by staying hydrated:

Water: Colour in the water bottles as you finish them

Getting enough sleep helps my brain face the day:

Tonight I will go to bed at: ____ pm

Date: ....

Today my anxiety level is: Low | Medium | High

I think that my anxiety today has been triggered by:

I plan to manage my anxiety today by using:

☐ Deep breathing   ☐ Grounding *(3 things)*

☐ Meditation   ☐ Aromatherapy

☐ Exercise   ☐ Talk Therapy

Three things I am proud of myself for today:

1)

2)

3)

Something that calmed me down today was:

What I would like to say to my 'Anxious Self' today:

This is what I would like my grown up's to know today:

HEALTHY BODY: HEALTHY MIND

Helping my body stay healthy, also helps my mind:

Today I supported my body & mind by staying hydrated:

Water: 🍼🍼🍼🍼🍼 Colour in the water bottles as you finish them

Getting enough sleep helps my brain face the day:

Tonight I will go to bed at: ___ pm

Date: ....

Today my anxiety level is: Low | Medium | High

I think that my anxiety today has been triggered by:

I plan to manage my anxiety today by using:

☐ Deep breathing   ☐ Grounding *(3 things)*

☐ Meditation   ☐ Aromatherapy

☐ Exercise   ☐ Talk Therapy

Three things I am proud of myself for today:

1)

2)

3)

Something that calmed me down today was:

What I would like to say to my 'Anxious Self' today:

This is what I would like my grown up's to know today:

HEALTHY BODY: HEALTHY MIND

Helping my body stay healthy, also helps my mind:

Today I supported my body & mind by staying hydrated:

Water: 🍼 🍼 🍼 🍼 🍼   Colour in the water bottles as you finish them

Getting enough sleep helps my brain face the day:

Tonight I will go to bed at: ____ pm

Date: ....

Today my anxiety level is: Low | Medium | High

I think that my anxiety today has been triggered by:

I plan to manage my anxiety today by using:

☐ Deep breathing   ☐ Grounding *(3 things)*

☐ Meditation   ☐ Aromatherapy

☐ Exercise   ☐ Talk Therapy

Three things I am proud of myself for today:

1)

2)

3)

Something that calmed me down today was:

What I would like to say to my 'Anxious Self' today:

This is what I would like my grown up's to know today:

HEALTHY BODY: HEALTHY MIND

Helping my body stay healthy, also helps my mind:

Today I supported my body & mind by staying hydrated:

Water: Colour in the water bottles as you finish them

Getting enough sleep helps my brain face the day:

Tonight I will go to bed at: ____ pm

Date: ....

Today my anxiety level is: Low | Medium | High

I think that my anxiety today has been triggered by:

I plan to manage my anxiety today by using:

☐ Deep breathing   ☐ Grounding (3 things)

☐ Meditation   ☐ Aromatherapy

☐ Exercise   ☐ Talk Therapy

Three things I am proud of myself for today:

1)

2)

3)

Something that calmed me down today was:

What I would like to say to my 'Anxious Self' today:

This is what I would like my grown up's to know today:

HEALTHY BODY: HEALTHY MIND

Helping my body stay healthy, also helps my mind:

Today I supported my body & mind by staying hydrated:

Water: Colour in the water bottles as you finish them

Getting enough sleep helps my brain face the day:

Tonight I will go to bed at: ___ pm

Date: ....

Today my anxiety level is: Low | Medium | High

I think that my anxiety today has been triggered by:

I plan to manage my anxiety today by using:

☐ Deep breathing   ☐ Grounding *(3 things)*

☐ Meditation   ☐ Aromatherapy

☐ Exercise   ☐ Talk Therapy

Three things I am proud of myself for today:

1)

2)

3)

Something that calmed me down today was:

What I would like to say to my 'Anxious Self' today:

This is what I would like my grown up's to know today:

HEALTHY BODY: HEALTHY MIND

Helping my body stay healthy, also helps my mind:

Today I supported my body & mind by staying hydrated:

Water: Colour in the water bottles as you finish them

Getting enough sleep helps my brain face the day:

Tonight I will go to bed at: ___ pm

Date: ....

Today my anxiety level is: Low | Medium | High

I think that my anxiety today has been triggered by:

I plan to manage my anxiety today by using:

☐ Deep breathing   ☐ Grounding *(3 things)*

☐ Meditation   ☐ Aromatherapy

☐ Exercise   ☐ Talk Therapy

Three things I am proud of myself for today:

1)

2)

3)

Something that calmed me down today was:

What I would like to say to my 'Anxious Self' today:

This is what I would like my grown up's to know today:

HEALTHY BODY: HEALTHY MIND

Helping my body stay healthy, also helps my mind:

Today I supported my body & mind by staying hydrated:

Water: [bottle] [bottle] [bottle] [bottle] [bottle]   Colour in the water bottles as you finish them

Getting enough sleep helps my brain face the day:

Tonight I will go to bed at: ____ pm

Date: ....

Today my anxiety level is: Low | Medium | High

I think that my anxiety today has been triggered by:

I plan to manage my anxiety today by using:

☐ Deep breathing   ☐ Grounding *(3 things)*

☐ Meditation   ☐ Aromatherapy

☐ Exercise   ☐ Talk Therapy

Three things I am proud of myself for today:

1)

2)

3)

Something that calmed me down today was:

What I would like to say to my 'Anxious Self' today:

This is what I would like my grown up's to know today:

HEALTHY BODY: HEALTHY MIND

Helping my body stay healthy, also helps my mind:

Today I supported my body & mind by staying hydrated:

Water: Colour in the water bottles as you finish them

Getting enough sleep helps my brain face the day:

Tonight I will go to bed at: ____ pm

Date: ....

Today my anxiety level is: Low | Medium | High

I think that my anxiety today has been triggered by:

I plan to manage my anxiety today by using:

☐ Deep breathing   ☐ Grounding *(3 things)*

☐ Meditation   ☐ Aromatherapy

☐ Exercise   ☐ Talk Therapy

Three things I am proud of myself for today:

1)

2)

3)

Something that calmed me down today was:

What I would like to say to my 'Anxious Self' today:

This is what I would like my grown up's to know today:

··► HEALTHY BODY: HEALTHY MIND ◄··

Helping my body stay healthy, also helps my mind:

Today I supported my body & mind by staying hydrated:

Water: ⌂⌂⌂⌂⌂   Colour in the water bottles as you finish them

Getting enough sleep helps my brain face the day:

Tonight I will go to bed at: ____ pm

Date: ....

Today my anxiety level is: Low | Medium | High

I think that my anxiety today has been triggered by:

I plan to manage my anxiety today by using:

☐ Deep breathing   ☐ Grounding *(3 things)*

☐ Meditation   ☐ Aromatherapy

☐ Exercise   ☐ Talk Therapy

Three things I am proud of myself for today:

1)

2)

3)

Something that calmed me down today was:

What I would like to say to my 'Anxious Self' today:

This is what I would like my grown up's to know today:

HEALTHY BODY: HEALTHY MIND

Helping my body stay healthy, also helps my mind:

Today I supported my body & mind by staying hydrated:

Water: Colour in the water bottles as you finish them

Getting enough sleep helps my brain face the day:

Tonight I will go to bed at: ____ pm

Date: ....

Today my anxiety level is: Low | Medium | High

I think that my anxiety today has been triggered by:

I plan to manage my anxiety today by using:

☐ Deep breathing   ☐ Grounding (3 things)

☐ Meditation   ☐ Aromatherapy

☐ Exercise   ☐ Talk Therapy

Three things I am proud of myself for today:

1)

2)

3)

Something that calmed me down today was:

What I would like to say to my 'Anxious Self' today:

This is what I would like my grown up's to know today:

HEALTHY BODY: HEALTHY MIND

Helping my body stay healthy, also helps my mind:

Today I supported my body & mind by staying hydrated:

Water: 〔〕〔〕〔〕〔〕〔〕   Colour in the water bottles as you finish them

Getting enough sleep helps my brain face the day:

Tonight I will go to bed at: ___ pm

Date: ....

Today my anxiety level is: Low | Medium | High

I think that my anxiety today has been triggered by:

I plan to manage my anxiety today by using:

☐ Deep breathing   ☐ Grounding *(3 things)*

☐ Meditation   ☐ Aromatherapy

☐ Exercise   ☐ Talk Therapy

Three things I am proud of myself for today:

1)

2)

3)

Something that calmed me down today was:

What I would like to say to my 'Anxious Self' today:

This is what I would like my grown up's to know today:

HEALTHY BODY: HEALTHY MIND

Helping my body stay healthy, also helps my mind:

Today I supported my body & mind by staying hydrated:

Water: Colour in the water bottles as you finish them

Getting enough sleep helps my brain face the day:

Tonight I will go to bed at: ____ pm

Date: ....

Today my anxiety level is: Low | Medium | High

I think that my anxiety today has been triggered by:

I plan to manage my anxiety today by using:

☐ Deep breathing   ☐ Grounding *(3 things)*

☐ Meditation   ☐ Aromatherapy

☐ Exercise   ☐ Talk Therapy

Three things I am proud of myself for today:

1)

2)

3)

Something that calmed me down today was:

What I would like to say to my 'Anxious Self' today:

This is what I would like my grown up's to know today:

HEALTHY BODY: HEALTHY MIND

Helping my body stay healthy, also helps my mind:

Today I supported my body & mind by staying hydrated:

Water: Colour in the water bottles as you finish them

Getting enough sleep helps my brain face the day:

Tonight I will go to bed at: ___ pm

Date: ....

Today my anxiety level is: Low | Medium | High

I think that my anxiety today has been triggered by:

I plan to manage my anxiety today by using:

☐ Deep breathing   ☐ Grounding *(3 things)*

☐ Meditation   ☐ Aromatherapy

☐ Exercise   ☐ Talk Therapy

Three things I am proud of myself for today:

1)

2)

3)

Something that calmed me down today was:

What I would like to say to my 'Anxious Self' today:

This is what I would like my grown up's to know today:

HEALTHY BODY: HEALTHY MIND

Helping my body stay healthy, also helps my mind:

Today I supported my body & mind by staying hydrated:

Water: Colour in the water bottles as you finish them

Getting enough sleep helps my brain face the day:

Tonight I will go to bed at: ____ pm

Date: ....

Today my anxiety level is: Low | Medium | High

I think that my anxiety today has been triggered by:

I plan to manage my anxiety today by using:

☐ Deep breathing   ☐ Grounding *(3 things)*

☐ Meditation   ☐ Aromatherapy

☐ Exercise   ☐ Talk Therapy

Three things I am proud of myself for today:

1)

2)

3)

Something that calmed me down today was:

What I would like to say to my 'Anxious Self' today:

This is what I would like my grown up's to know today:

HEALTHY BODY: HEALTHY MIND

Helping my body stay healthy, also helps my mind:

Today I supported my body & mind by staying hydrated:

Water: Colour in the water bottles as you finish them

Getting enough sleep helps my brain face the day:

Tonight I will go to bed at: ____ pm

Date:

Today my anxiety level is: Low | Medium | High

I think that my anxiety today has been triggered by:

I plan to manage my anxiety today by using:

☐ Deep breathing   ☐ Grounding *(3 things)*

☐ Meditation   ☐ Aromatherapy

☐ Exercise   ☐ Talk Therapy

Three things I am proud of myself for today:

1)

2)

3)

Something that calmed me down today was:

What I would like to say to my 'Anxious Self' today:

This is what I would like my grown up's to know today:

HEALTHY BODY: HEALTHY MIND

Helping my body stay healthy, also helps my mind:

Today I supported my body & mind by staying hydrated:

Water: [bottle] [bottle] [bottle] [bottle] [bottle]   Colour in the water bottles as you finish them

Getting enough sleep helps my brain face the day:

Tonight I will go to bed at: ＿＿＿ pm

Date: ....

Today my anxiety level is: Low | Medium | High

I think that my anxiety today has been triggered by:

I plan to manage my anxiety today by using:

☐ Deep breathing	☐ Grounding *(3 things)*	
☐ Meditation	☐ Aromatherapy	
☐ Exercise	☐ Talk Therapy	

Three things I am proud of myself for today:

1)

2)

3)

Something that calmed me down today was:

What I would like to say to my 'Anxious Self' today:

This is what I would like my grown up's to know today:

HEALTHY BODY: HEALTHY MIND

Helping my body stay healthy, also helps my mind:

Today I supported my body & mind by staying hydrated:

Water: 🍼 🍼 🍼 🍼 🍼   Colour in the water bottles as you finish them

Getting enough sleep helps my brain face the day:

Tonight I will go to bed at: ____ pm

Date: ....

Today my anxiety level is: Low | Medium | High

I think that my anxiety today has been triggered by:

I plan to manage my anxiety today by using:

☐ Deep breathing   ☐ Grounding *(3 things)*

☐ Meditation   ☐ Aromatherapy

☐ Exercise   ☐ Talk Therapy

Three things I am proud of myself for today:

1)

2)

3)

Something that calmed me down today was:

What I would like to say to my 'Anxious Self' today:

This is what I would like my grown up's to know today:

HEALTHY BODY: HEALTHY MIND

Helping my body stay healthy, also helps my mind:

Today I supported my body & mind by staying hydrated:

Water: [ ] [ ] [ ] [ ] [ ]   Colour in the water bottles as you finish them

Getting enough sleep helps my brain face the day:

Tonight I will go to bed at: ____ pm

Date: ....

Today my anxiety level is: Low | Medium | High

I think that my anxiety today has been triggered by:

I plan to manage my anxiety today by using:

☐ Deep breathing   ☐ Grounding *(3 things)*

☐ Meditation   ☐ Aromatherapy

☐ Exercise   ☐ Talk Therapy

Three things I am proud of myself for today:

1)

2)

3)

Something that calmed me down today was:

What I would like to say to my 'Anxious Self' today:

This is what I would like my grown up's to know today:

HEALTHY BODY: HEALTHY MIND

Helping my body stay healthy, also helps my mind:

Today I supported my body & mind by staying hydrated:

Water: Colour in the water bottles as you finish them

Getting enough sleep helps my brain face the day:

Tonight I will go to bed at: ____ pm

Date: ....

Today my anxiety level is: Low | Medium | High

I think that my anxiety today has been triggered by:

I plan to manage my anxiety today by using:

☐	Deep breathing	☐	Grounding *(3 things)*
☐	Meditation	☐	Aromatherapy
☐	Exercise	☐	Talk Therapy

Three things I am proud of myself for today:

1)

2)

3)

Something that calmed me down today was:

What I would like to say to my 'Anxious Self' today:

This is what I would like my grown up's to know today:

HEALTHY BODY: HEALTHY MIND

Helping my body stay healthy, also helps my mind:

Today I supported my body & mind by staying hydrated:

Water: Colour in the water bottles as you finish them

Getting enough sleep helps my brain face the day:

Tonight I will go to bed at: ____ pm

Date: ....

Today my anxiety level is: Low | Medium | High

I think that my anxiety today has been triggered by:

I plan to manage my anxiety today by using:

☐ Deep breathing   ☐ Grounding *(3 things)*

☐ Meditation   ☐ Aromatherapy

☐ Exercise   ☐ Talk Therapy

Three things I am proud of myself for today:

1)

2)

3)

Something that calmed me down today was:

What I would like to say to my 'Anxious Self' today:

This is what I would like my grown up's to know today:

HEALTHY BODY: HEALTHY MIND

Helping my body stay healthy, also helps my mind:

Today I supported my body & mind by staying hydrated:

Water: Colour in the water bottles as you finish them

Getting enough sleep helps my brain face the day:

Tonight I will go to bed at: ____ pm

Date: ....

Today my anxiety level is: Low | Medium | High

I think that my anxiety today has been triggered by:

I plan to manage my anxiety today by using:

☐ Deep breathing   ☐ Grounding *(3 things)*

☐ Meditation   ☐ Aromatherapy

☐ Exercise   ☐ Talk Therapy

Three things I am proud of myself for today:

1)

2)

3)

Something that calmed me down today was:

What I would like to say to my 'Anxious Self' today:

This is what I would like my grown up's to know today:

HEALTHY BODY: HEALTHY MIND

Helping my body stay healthy, also helps my mind:

Today I supported my body & mind by staying hydrated:

Water: 🍼🍼🍼🍼🍼 Colour in the water bottles as you finish them

Getting enough sleep helps my brain face the day:

Tonight I will go to bed at: ___ pm

Date: ....

Today my anxiety level is: Low | Medium | High

I think that my anxiety today has been triggered by:

I plan to manage my anxiety today by using:

☐ Deep breathing   ☐ Grounding *(3 things)*

☐ Meditation   ☐ Aromatherapy

☐ Exercise   ☐ Talk Therapy

Three things I am proud of myself for today:

1)

2)

3)

Something that calmed me down today was:

What I would like to say to my 'Anxious Self' today:

This is what I would like my grown up's to know today:

HEALTHY BODY: HEALTHY MIND

Helping my body stay healthy, also helps my mind:

Today I supported my body & mind by staying hydrated:

Water: 🍼🍼🍼🍼🍼 Colour in the water bottles as you finish them

Getting enough sleep helps my brain face the day:

Tonight I will go to bed at: ____ pm

Date: ....

Today my anxiety level is: Low | Medium | High

I think that my anxiety today has been triggered by:

I plan to manage my anxiety today by using:

☐ Deep breathing   ☐ Grounding *(3 things)*

☐ Meditation   ☐ Aromatherapy

☐ Exercise   ☐ Talk Therapy

Three things I am proud of myself for today:

1)

2)

3)

Something that calmed me down today was:

What I would like to say to my 'Anxious Self' today:

This is what I would like my grown up's to know today:

························➤ HEALTHY BODY: HEALTHY MIND ◄························

Helping my body stay healthy, also helps my mind:

Today I supported my body & mind by staying hydrated:

Water: 🍼 🍼 🍼 🍼 🍼   Colour in the water bottles as you finish them

Getting enough sleep helps my brain face the day:

Tonight I will go to bed at: ____ pm

Date: ....

Today my anxiety level is: Low | Medium | High

I think that my anxiety today has been triggered by:

I plan to manage my anxiety today by using:

☐ Deep breathing   ☐ Grounding *(3 things)*

☐ Meditation   ☐ Aromatherapy

☐ Exercise   ☐ Talk Therapy

Three things I am proud of myself for today:

1)

2)

3)

Something that calmed me down today was:

What I would like to say to my 'Anxious Self' today:

This is what I would like my grown up's to know today:

HEALTHY BODY: HEALTHY MIND

Helping my body stay healthy, also helps my mind:

Today I supported my body & mind by staying hydrated:

Water: Colour in the water bottles as you finish them

Getting enough sleep helps my brain face the day:

Tonight I will go to bed at: ____ pm

Date: ....

Today my anxiety level is: Low | Medium | High

I think that my anxiety today has been triggered by:

I plan to manage my anxiety today by using:

- [ ] Deep breathing
- [ ] Meditation
- [ ] Exercise

- [ ] Grounding (3 things)
- [ ] Aromatherapy
- [ ] Talk Therapy

Three things I am proud of myself for today:

1)

2)

3)

Something that calmed me down today was:

What I would like to say to my 'Anxious Self' today:

This is what I would like my grown up's to know today:

HEALTHY BODY: HEALTHY MIND

Helping my body stay healthy, also helps my mind:

Today I supported my body & mind by staying hydrated:

Water: Colour in the water bottles as you finish them

Getting enough sleep helps my brain face the day:

Tonight I will go to bed at: ____ pm

Date: ....

Today my anxiety level is: Low | Medium | High

I think that my anxiety today has been triggered by:

I plan to manage my anxiety today by using:

☐ Deep breathing   ☐ Grounding *(3 things)*

☐ Meditation   ☐ Aromatherapy

☐ Exercise   ☐ Talk Therapy

Three things I am proud of myself for today:

1)

2)

3)

Something that calmed me down today was:

What I would like to say to my 'Anxious Self' today:

This is what I would like my grown up's to know today:

HEALTHY BODY: HEALTHY MIND

Helping my body stay healthy, also helps my mind:

Today I supported my body & mind by staying hydrated:

Water: ⌂⌂⌂⌂⌂ Colour in the water bottles as you finish them

Getting enough sleep helps my brain face the day:

Tonight I will go to bed at: ___ pm

Date: ....

Today my anxiety level is: Low | Medium | High

I think that my anxiety today has been triggered by:

I plan to manage my anxiety today by using:

☐ Deep breathing ☐ Grounding *(3 things)*

☐ Meditation ☐ Aromatherapy

☐ Exercise ☐ Talk Therapy

Three things I am proud of myself for today:

1)

2)

3)

Something that calmed me down today was:

What I would like to say to my 'Anxious Self' today:

This is what I would like my grown up's to know today:

HEALTHY BODY: HEALTHY MIND

Helping my body stay healthy, also helps my mind:

Today I supported my body & mind by staying hydrated:

Water: Colour in the water bottles as you finish them

Getting enough sleep helps my brain face the day:

Tonight I will go to bed at: ____ pm

Date: ....

Today my anxiety level is: Low | Medium | High

I think that my anxiety today has been triggered by:

I plan to manage my anxiety today by using:

☐ Deep breathing   ☐ Grounding *(3 things)*

☐ Meditation   ☐ Aromatherapy

☐ Exercise   ☐ Talk Therapy

Three things I am proud of myself for today:

1)

2)

3)

Something that calmed me down today was:

What I would like to say to my 'Anxious Self' today:

This is what I would like my grown up's to know today:

HEALTHY BODY: HEALTHY MIND

Helping my body stay healthy, also helps my mind:

Today I supported my body & mind by staying hydrated:

Water: 🍼🍼🍼🍼🍼   Colour in the water bottles as you finish them

Getting enough sleep helps my brain face the day:

Tonight I will go to bed at: ___ pm

Date: ....

Today my anxiety level is: Low | Medium | High

I think that my anxiety today has been triggered by:

I plan to manage my anxiety today by using:

☐ Deep breathing   ☐ Grounding *(3 things)*

☐ Meditation   ☐ Aromatherapy

☐ Exercise   ☐ Talk Therapy

Three things I am proud of myself for today:

1)

2)

3)

Something that calmed me down today was:

What I would like to say to my 'Anxious Self' today:

This is what I would like my grown up's to know today:

HEALTHY BODY: HEALTHY MIND

Helping my body stay healthy, also helps my mind:

Today I supported my body & mind by staying hydrated:

Water: Colour in the water bottles as you finish them

Getting enough sleep helps my brain face the day:

Tonight I will go to bed at: ____ pm

Date: ....

Today my anxiety level is: Low | Medium | High

I think that my anxiety today has been triggered by:

I plan to manage my anxiety today by using:

☐ Deep breathing   ☐ Grounding *(3 things)*

☐ Meditation   ☐ Aromatherapy

☐ Exercise   ☐ Talk Therapy

Three things I am proud of myself for today:

1)

2)

3)

Something that calmed me down today was:

What I would like to say to my 'Anxious Self' today:

This is what I would like my grown up's to know today:

HEALTHY BODY: HEALTHY MIND

Helping my body stay healthy, also helps my mind:

Today I supported my body & mind by staying hydrated:

Water: Colour in the water bottles as you finish them

Getting enough sleep helps my brain face the day:

Tonight I will go to bed at: ____ pm

Date: ....

Today my anxiety level is: Low | Medium | High

I think that my anxiety today has been triggered by:

I plan to manage my anxiety today by using:

☐ Deep breathing   ☐ Grounding *(3 things)*

☐ Meditation   ☐ Aromatherapy

☐ Exercise   ☐ Talk Therapy

Three things I am proud of myself for today:

1)

2)

3)

Something that calmed me down today was:

What I would like to say to my 'Anxious Self' today:

This is what I would like my grown up's to know today:

················→ HEALTHY BODY: HEALTHY MIND ·····················→

Helping my body stay healthy, also helps my mind:

Today I supported my body & mind by staying hydrated:

Water: Colour in the water bottles as you finish them

Getting enough sleep helps my brain face the day:

Tonight I will go to bed at: ____ pm

Date: ....

Today my anxiety level is: Low | Medium | High

I think that my anxiety today has been triggered by:

I plan to manage my anxiety today by using:

☐ Deep breathing   ☐ Grounding *(3 things)*

☐ Meditation   ☐ Aromatherapy

☐ Exercise   ☐ Talk Therapy

Three things I am proud of myself for today:

1)

2)

3)

Something that calmed me down today was:

What I would like to say to my 'Anxious Self' today:

This is what I would like my grown up's to know today:

Helping my body stay healthy, also helps my mind:

Today I supported my body & mind by staying hydrated:

Water: Colour in the water bottles as you finish them

Getting enough sleep helps my brain face the day:

Tonight I will go to bed at: ___ pm

Date:

Today my anxiety level is: Low | Medium | High

I think that my anxiety today has been triggered by:

I plan to manage my anxiety today by using:

- [ ] Deep breathing
- [ ] Meditation
- [ ] Exercise
- [ ] Grounding *(3 things)*
- [ ] Aromatherapy
- [ ] Talk Therapy

Three things I am proud of myself for today:

1)

2)

3)

Something that calmed me down today was:

What I would like to say to my 'Anxious Self' today:

This is what I would like my grown up's to know today:

HEALTHY BODY: HEALTHY MIND

Helping my body stay healthy, also helps my mind:

Today I supported my body & mind by staying hydrated:

Water: 🍼🍼🍼🍼🍼 Colour in the water bottles as you finish them

Getting enough sleep helps my brain face the day:

Tonight I will go to bed at: ____ pm

Date: ....

Today my anxiety level is: Low | Medium | High

I think that my anxiety today has been triggered by:

I plan to manage my anxiety today by using:

☐   Deep breathing   ☐   Grounding *(3 things)*

☐   Meditation   ☐   Aromatherapy

☐   Exercise   ☐   Talk Therapy

Three things I am proud of myself for today:

1)

2)

3)

Something that calmed me down today was:

What I would like to say to my 'Anxious Self' today:

This is what I would like my grown up's to know today:

HEALTHY BODY: HEALTHY MIND

Helping my body stay healthy, also helps my mind:

Today I supported my body & mind by staying hydrated:

Water: Colour in the water bottles as you finish them

Getting enough sleep helps my brain face the day:

Tonight I will go to bed at: ___ pm

Date: ....

Today my anxiety level is: Low | Medium | High

I think that my anxiety today has been triggered by:

I plan to manage my anxiety today by using:

☐ Deep breathing   ☐ Grounding *(3 things)*

☐ Meditation   ☐ Aromatherapy

☐ Exercise   ☐ Talk Therapy

Three things I am proud of myself for today:

1)

2)

3)

Something that calmed me down today was:

What I would like to say to my 'Anxious Self' today:

This is what I would like my grown up's to know today:

HEALTHY BODY: HEALTHY MIND

Helping my body stay healthy, also helps my mind:

Today I supported my body & mind by staying hydrated:

Water: Colour in the water bottles as you finish them

Getting enough sleep helps my brain face the day:

Tonight I will go to bed at: ____ pm

Date: ....

Today my anxiety level is: Low | Medium | High

I think that my anxiety today has been triggered by:

I plan to manage my anxiety today by using:

☐ Deep breathing   ☐ Grounding *(3 things)*

☐ Meditation   ☐ Aromatherapy

☐ Exercise   ☐ Talk Therapy

Three things I am proud of myself for today:

1)

2)

3)

Something that calmed me down today was:

What I would like to say to my 'Anxious Self' today:

This is what I would like my grown up's to know today:

HEALTHY BODY: HEALTHY MIND

Helping my body stay healthy, also helps my mind:

Today I supported my body & mind by staying hydrated:

Water: Colour in the water bottles as you finish them

Getting enough sleep helps my brain face the day:

Tonight I will go to bed at: ____ pm

Date: _____

Today my anxiety level is: Low | Medium | High

I think that my anxiety today has been triggered by:

I plan to manage my anxiety today by using:

☐ Deep breathing   ☐ Grounding *(3 things)*

☐ Meditation   ☐ Aromatherapy

☐ Exercise   ☐ Talk Therapy

Three things I am proud of myself for today:

1)

2)

3)

Something that calmed me down today was:

What I would like to say to my 'Anxious Self' today:

This is what I would like my grown up's to know today:

HEALTHY BODY: HEALTHY MIND

Helping my body stay healthy, also helps my mind:

Today I supported my body & mind by staying hydrated:

Water: 🍼🍼🍼🍼🍼   Colour in the water bottles as you finish them

Getting enough sleep helps my brain face the day:

Tonight I will go to bed at: ____ pm

Date: ....

Today my anxiety level is: Low | Medium | High

I think that my anxiety today has been triggered by:

I plan to manage my anxiety today by using:

☐ Deep breathing   ☐ Grounding *(3 things)*

☐ Meditation   ☐ Aromatherapy

☐ Exercise   ☐ Talk Therapy

Three things I am proud of myself for today:

1)

2)

3)

Something that calmed me down today was:

What I would like to say to my 'Anxious Self' today:

This is what I would like my grown up's to know today:

······· HEALTHY BODY: HEALTHY MIND ·······

Helping my body stay healthy, also helps my mind:

Today I supported my body & mind by staying hydrated:

Water: ⚬ ⚬ ⚬ ⚬ ⚬   Colour in the water bottles as you finish them

Getting enough sleep helps my brain face the day:

Tonight I will go to bed at: ____ pm

Date: ....

Today my anxiety level is: Low | Medium | High

I think that my anxiety today has been triggered by:

I plan to manage my anxiety today by using:

☐ Deep breathing   ☐ Grounding *(3 things)*

☐ Meditation   ☐ Aromatherapy

☐ Exercise   ☐ Talk Therapy

Three things I am proud of myself for today:

1)

2)

3)

Something that calmed me down today was:

What I would like to say to my 'Anxious Self' today:

This is what I would like my grown up's to know today:

HEALTHY BODY: HEALTHY MIND

Helping my body stay healthy, also helps my mind:

Today I supported my body & mind by staying hydrated:

Water: Colour in the water bottles as you finish them

Getting enough sleep helps my brain face the day:

Tonight I will go to bed at: ____ pm

Date: ....

Today my anxiety level is: Low | Medium | High

I think that my anxiety today has been triggered by:

I plan to manage my anxiety today by using:

☐ Deep breathing ☐ Grounding *(3 things)*

☐ Meditation ☐ Aromatherapy

☐ Exercise ☐ Talk Therapy

Three things I am proud of myself for today:

1)

2)

3)

Something that calmed me down today was:

What I would like to say to my 'Anxious Self' today:

This is what I would like my grown up's to know today:

HEALTHY BODY: HEALTHY MIND

Helping my body stay healthy, also helps my mind:

Today I supported my body & mind by staying hydrated:

Water: ⌂ ⌂ ⌂ ⌂ ⌂   Colour in the water bottles as you finish them

Getting enough sleep helps my brain face the day:

Tonight I will go to bed at: ___ pm

Date: ....

Today my anxiety level is: Low | Medium | High

I think that my anxiety today has been triggered by:

I plan to manage my anxiety today by using:

☐ Deep breathing ☐ Grounding *(3 things)*

☐ Meditation ☐ Aromatherapy

☐ Exercise ☐ Talk Therapy

Three things I am proud of myself for today:

1)

2)

3)

Something that calmed me down today was:

What I would like to say to my 'Anxious Self' today:

This is what I would like my grown up's to know today:

HEALTHY BODY: HEALTHY MIND

Helping my body stay healthy, also helps my mind:

Today I supported my body & mind by staying hydrated:

Water: Colour in the water bottles as you finish them

Getting enough sleep helps my brain face the day:

Tonight I will go to bed at: ____ pm

Date: ....

Today my anxiety level is: Low | Medium | High

I think that my anxiety today has been triggered by:

I plan to manage my anxiety today by using:

☐ Deep breathing   ☐ Grounding (3 things)

☐ Meditation   ☐ Aromatherapy

☐ Exercise   ☐ Talk Therapy

Three things I am proud of myself for today:

1)

2)

3)

Something that calmed me down today was:

What I would like to say to my 'Anxious Self' today:

This is what I would like my grown up's to know today:

HEALTHY BODY: HEALTHY MIND

Helping my body stay healthy, also helps my mind:

Today I supported my body & mind by staying hydrated:

Water: (water bottles)   Colour in the water bottles as you finish them

Getting enough sleep helps my brain face the day:

Tonight I will go to bed at: ____ pm

Date: ....

Today my anxiety level is: Low | Medium | High

I think that my anxiety today has been triggered by:

I plan to manage my anxiety today by using:

☐ Deep breathing   ☐ Grounding *(3 things)*

☐ Meditation   ☐ Aromatherapy

☐ Exercise   ☐ Talk Therapy

Three things I am proud of myself for today:

1)

2)

3)

Something that calmed me down today was:

What I would like to say to my 'Anxious Self' today:

This is what I would like my grown up's to know today:

HEALTHY BODY: HEALTHY MIND

Helping my body stay healthy, also helps my mind:

Today I supported my body & mind by staying hydrated:

Water: Colour in the water bottles as you finish them

Getting enough sleep helps my brain face the day:

Tonight I will go to bed at: ____ pm

Date: ....

Today my anxiety level is: Low | Medium | High

I think that my anxiety today has been triggered by:

I plan to manage my anxiety today by using:

☐ Deep breathing   ☐ Grounding *(3 things)*

☐ Meditation   ☐ Aromatherapy

☐ Exercise   ☐ Talk Therapy

Three things I am proud of myself for today:

1)

2)

3)

Something that calmed me down today was:

What I would like to say to my 'Anxious Self' today:

This is what I would like my grown up's to know today:

HEALTHY BODY: HEALTHY MIND

Helping my body stay healthy, also helps my mind:

Today I supported my body & mind by staying hydrated:

Water: Colour in the water bottles as you finish them

Getting enough sleep helps my brain face the day:

Tonight I will go to bed at: ____ pm

Date: ....

Today my anxiety level is: Low | Medium | High

I think that my anxiety today has been triggered by:

I plan to manage my anxiety today by using:

☐ Deep breathing   ☐ Grounding *(3 things)*

☐ Meditation   ☐ Aromatherapy

☐ Exercise   ☐ Talk Therapy

Three things I am proud of myself for today:

1)

2)

3)

Something that calmed me down today was:

What I would like to say to my 'Anxious Self' today:

This is what I would like my grown up's to know today:

HEALTHY BODY: HEALTHY MIND

Helping my body stay healthy, also helps my mind:

Today I supported my body & mind by staying hydrated:

Water: Colour in the water bottles as you finish them

Getting enough sleep helps my brain face the day:

Tonight I will go to bed at: ____ pm

Date:

Today my anxiety level is: Low | Medium | High

I think that my anxiety today has been triggered by:

I plan to manage my anxiety today by using:

☐ Deep breathing   ☐ Grounding *(3 things)*

☐ Meditation   ☐ Aromatherapy

☐ Exercise   ☐ Talk Therapy

Three things I am proud of myself for today:

1)

2)

3)

Something that calmed me down today was:

What I would like to say to my 'Anxious Self' today:

This is what I would like my grown up's to know today:

HEALTHY BODY: HEALTHY MIND

Helping my body stay healthy, also helps my mind:

Today I supported my body & mind by staying hydrated:

Water: 🍼🍼🍼🍼🍼   Colour in the water bottles as you finish them

Getting enough sleep helps my brain face the day:

Tonight I will go to bed at: ___ pm

Date: ....

Today my anxiety level is: Low | Medium | High

I think that my anxiety today has been triggered by:

I plan to manage my anxiety today by using:

☐ Deep breathing   ☐ Grounding *(3 things)*

☐ Meditation   ☐ Aromatherapy

☐ Exercise   ☐ Talk Therapy

Three things I am proud of myself for today:

1)

2)

3)

Something that calmed me down today was:

What I would like to say to my 'Anxious Self' today:

This is what I would like my grown up's to know today:

HEALTHY BODY: HEALTHY MIND

Helping my body stay healthy, also helps my mind:

Today I supported my body & mind by staying hydrated:

Water: Colour in the water bottles as you finish them

Getting enough sleep helps my brain face the day:

Tonight I will go to bed at: ____ pm

Date: ....

Today my anxiety level is: Low | Medium | High

I think that my anxiety today has been triggered by:

I plan to manage my anxiety today by using:

☐ Deep breathing   ☐ Grounding *(3 things)*

☐ Meditation   ☐ Aromatherapy

☐ Exercise   ☐ Talk Therapy

Three things I am proud of myself for today:

1)

2)

3)

Something that calmed me down today was:

What I would like to say to my 'Anxious Self' today:

This is what I would like my grown up's to know today:

············→ HEALTHY BODY: HEALTHY MIND ←············

Helping my body stay healthy, also helps my mind:

Today I supported my body & mind by staying hydrated:

Water: ⛶ ⛶ ⛶ ⛶ ⛶   Colour in the water bottles as you finish them

Getting enough sleep helps my brain face the day:

Tonight I will go to bed at: ____ pm

Date: ....

Today my anxiety level is: Low | Medium | High

I think that my anxiety today has been triggered by:

I plan to manage my anxiety today by using:

| | Deep breathing | | Grounding *(3 things)* |

| | Meditation | | Aromatherapy |

| | Exercise | | Talk Therapy |

Three things I am proud of myself for today:

1)

2)

3)

Something that calmed me down today was:

What I would like to say to my 'Anxious Self' today:

This is what I would like my grown up's to know today:

HEALTHY BODY: HEALTHY MIND

Helping my body stay healthy, also helps my mind:

Today I supported my body & mind by staying hydrated:

Water: Colour in the water bottles as you finish them

Getting enough sleep helps my brain face the day:

Tonight I will go to bed at: ___ pm

Date: ....

Today my anxiety level is: Low | Medium | High

I think that my anxiety today has been triggered by:

I plan to manage my anxiety today by using:

☐ Deep breathing   ☐ Grounding *(3 things)*

☐ Meditation   ☐ Aromatherapy

☐ Exercise   ☐ Talk Therapy

Three things I am proud of myself for today:

1)

2)

3)

Something that calmed me down today was:

What I would like to say to my 'Anxious Self' today:

This is what I would like my grown up's to know today:

Helping my body stay healthy, also helps my mind:

Today I supported my body & mind by staying hydrated:

Water: 　Colour in the water bottles as you finish them

Getting enough sleep helps my brain face the day:

Tonight I will go to bed at: ____ pm

Date: ....

Today my anxiety level is: Low | Medium | High

I think that my anxiety today has been triggered by:

I plan to manage my anxiety today by using:

☐ Deep breathing   ☐ Grounding *(3 things)*

☐ Meditation   ☐ Aromatherapy

☐ Exercise   ☐ Talk Therapy

Three things I am proud of myself for today:

1)

2)

3)

Something that calmed me down today was:

What I would like to say to my 'Anxious Self' today:

This is what I would like my grown up's to know today:

HEALTHY BODY: HEALTHY MIND

Helping my body stay healthy, also helps my mind:

Today I supported my body & mind by staying hydrated:

Water: Colour in the water bottles as you finish them

Getting enough sleep helps my brain face the day:

Tonight I will go to bed at: ____ pm

Date: ....

Today my anxiety level is: Low | Medium | High

I think that my anxiety today has been triggered by:

I plan to manage my anxiety today by using:

☐ Deep breathing   ☐ Grounding *(3 things)*

☐ Meditation   ☐ Aromatherapy

☐ Exercise   ☐ Talk Therapy

Three things I am proud of myself for today:

1)

2)

3)

Something that calmed me down today was:

What I would like to say to my 'Anxious Self' today:

This is what I would like my grown up's to know today:

HEALTHY BODY: HEALTHY MIND

Helping my body stay healthy, also helps my mind:

Today I supported my body & mind by staying hydrated:

Water: Colour in the water bottles as you finish them

Getting enough sleep helps my brain face the day:

Tonight I will go to bed at: ____ pm

Date: ....

Today my anxiety level is: Low | Medium | High

I think that my anxiety today has been triggered by:

I plan to manage my anxiety today by using:

☐ Deep breathing   ☐ Grounding (3 things)

☐ Meditation   ☐ Aromatherapy

☐ Exercise   ☐ Talk Therapy

Three things I am proud of myself for today:

1)

2)

3)

Something that calmed me down today was:

What I would like to say to my 'Anxious Self' today:

This is what I would like my grown up's to know today:

HEALTHY BODY: HEALTHY MIND

Helping my body stay healthy, also helps my mind:

Today I supported my body & mind by staying hydrated:

Water: Colour in the water bottles as you finish them

Getting enough sleep helps my brain face the day:

Tonight I will go to bed at: ____ pm

Date:

Today my anxiety level is: Low | Medium | High

I think that my anxiety today has been triggered by:

I plan to manage my anxiety today by using:

☐ Deep breathing   ☐ Grounding *(3 things)*

☐ Meditation   ☐ Aromatherapy

☐ Exercise   ☐ Talk Therapy

Three things I am proud of myself for today:

1)

2)

3)

Something that calmed me down today was:

What I would like to say to my 'Anxious Self' today:

This is what I would like my grown up's to know today:

HEALTHY BODY: HEALTHY MIND

Helping my body stay healthy, also helps my mind:

Today I supported my body & mind by staying hydrated:

Water: Colour in the water bottles as you finish them

Getting enough sleep helps my brain face the day:

Tonight I will go to bed at: ____ pm

Date: ....

Today my anxiety level is: Low | Medium | High

I think that my anxiety today has been triggered by:

I plan to manage my anxiety today by using:

☐ Deep breathing   ☐ Grounding (3 things)

☐ Meditation   ☐ Aromatherapy

☐ Exercise   ☐ Talk Therapy

Three things I am proud of myself for today:

1)

2)

3)

Something that calmed me down today was:

What I would like to say to my 'Anxious Self' today:

This is what I would like my grown up's to know today:

HEALTHY BODY: HEALTHY MIND

Helping my body stay healthy, also helps my mind:

Today I supported my body & mind by staying hydrated:

Water: Colour in the water bottles as you finish them

Getting enough sleep helps my brain face the day:

Tonight I will go to bed at: ___ pm

Date: ....

Today my anxiety level is: Low | Medium | High

I think that my anxiety today has been triggered by:

I plan to manage my anxiety today by using:

☐ Deep breathing   ☐ Grounding *(3 things)*

☐ Meditation   ☐ Aromatherapy

☐ Exercise   ☐ Talk Therapy

Three things I am proud of myself for today:

1)

2)

3)

Something that calmed me down today was:

What I would like to say to my 'Anxious Self' today:

This is what I would like my grown up's to know today:

HEALTHY BODY: HEALTHY MIND

Helping my body stay healthy, also helps my mind:

Today I supported my body & mind by staying hydrated:

Water: Colour in the water bottles as you finish them

Getting enough sleep helps my brain face the day:

Tonight I will go to bed at: ____ pm

Date: ....

Today my anxiety level is: Low | Medium | High

I think that my anxiety today has been triggered by:

I plan to manage my anxiety today by using:

☐ Deep breathing   ☐ Grounding *(3 things)*

☐ Meditation   ☐ Aromatherapy

☐ Exercise   ☐ Talk Therapy

Three things I am proud of myself for today:

1)

2)

3)

Something that calmed me down today was:

What I would like to say to my 'Anxious Self' today:

This is what I would like my grown up's to know today:

HEALTHY BODY: HEALTHY MIND

Helping my body stay healthy, also helps my mind:

Today I supported my body & mind by staying hydrated:

Water: Colour in the water bottles as you finish them

Getting enough sleep helps my brain face the day:

Tonight I will go to bed at: ____ pm

Date: ....

Today my anxiety level is: Low | Medium | High

I think that my anxiety today has been triggered by:

I plan to manage my anxiety today by using:

☐ Deep breathing   ☐ Grounding *(3 things)*

☐ Meditation   ☐ Aromatherapy

☐ Exercise   ☐ Talk Therapy

Three things I am proud of myself for today:

1)

2)

3)

Something that calmed me down today was:

What I would like to say to my 'Anxious Self' today:

This is what I would like my grown up's to know today:

HEALTHY BODY: HEALTHY MIND

Helping my body stay healthy, also helps my mind:

Today I supported my body & mind by staying hydrated:

Water: Colour in the water bottles as you finish them

Getting enough sleep helps my brain face the day:

Tonight I will go to bed at: ___ pm

Date: ....

Today my anxiety level is: Low | Medium | High

I think that my anxiety today has been triggered by:

I plan to manage my anxiety today by using:

☐ Deep breathing   ☐ Grounding *(3 things)*

☐ Meditation   ☐ Aromatherapy

☐ Exercise   ☐ Talk Therapy

Three things I am proud of myself for today:

1)

2)

3)

Something that calmed me down today was:

What I would like to say to my 'Anxious Self' today:

This is what I would like my grown up's to know today:

HEALTHY BODY: HEALTHY MIND

Helping my body stay healthy, also helps my mind:

Today I supported my body & mind by staying hydrated:

Water: ⛶ ⛶ ⛶ ⛶ ⛶   Colour in the water bottles as you finish them

Getting enough sleep helps my brain face the day:

Tonight I will go to bed at: ____ pm

Date: ....

Today my anxiety level is: Low | Medium | High

I think that my anxiety today has been triggered by:

I plan to manage my anxiety today by using:

☐ Deep breathing   ☐ Grounding *(3 things)*

☐ Meditation   ☐ Aromatherapy

☐ Exercise   ☐ Talk Therapy

Three things I am proud of myself for today:

1)

2)

3)

Something that calmed me down today was:

What I would like to say to my 'Anxious Self' today:

This is what I would like my grown up's to know today:

HEALTHY BODY: HEALTHY MIND

Helping my body stay healthy, also helps my mind:

Today I supported my body & mind by staying hydrated:

Water: [bottle] [bottle] [bottle] [bottle] [bottle]   Colour in the water bottles as you finish them

Getting enough sleep helps my brain face the day:

Tonight I will go to bed at: ____ pm

Date: ....

Today my anxiety level is: Low | Medium | High

I think that my anxiety today has been triggered by:

I plan to manage my anxiety today by using:

☐ Deep breathing   ☐ Grounding *(3 things)*

☐ Meditation   ☐ Aromatherapy

☐ Exercise   ☐ Talk Therapy

Three things I am proud of myself for today:

1)

2)

3)

Something that calmed me down today was:

What I would like to say to my 'Anxious Self' today:

This is what I would like my grown up's to know today:

HEALTHY BODY: HEALTHY MIND

Helping my body stay healthy, also helps my mind:

Today I supported my body & mind by staying hydrated:

Water: Colour in the water bottles as you finish them

Getting enough sleep helps my brain face the day:

Tonight I will go to bed at: ____ pm

Date: ....

Today my anxiety level is: Low | Medium | High

I think that my anxiety today has been triggered by:

I plan to manage my anxiety today by using:

☐ Deep breathing   ☐ Grounding *(3 things)*

☐ Meditation   ☐ Aromatherapy

☐ Exercise   ☐ Talk Therapy

Three things I am proud of myself for today:

1)

2)

3)

Something that calmed me down today was:

What I would like to say to my 'Anxious Self' today:

This is what I would like my grown up's to know today:

HEALTHY BODY: HEALTHY MIND

Helping my body stay healthy, also helps my mind:

Today I supported my body & mind by staying hydrated:

Water: Colour in the water bottles as you finish them

Getting enough sleep helps my brain face the day:

Tonight I will go to bed at: ____ pm

Date: ....

Today my anxiety level is: Low | Medium | High

I think that my anxiety today has been triggered by:

I plan to manage my anxiety today by using:

☐ Deep breathing   ☐ Grounding *(3 things)*

☐ Meditation   ☐ Aromatherapy

☐ Exercice   ☐ Talk Therapy

Three things I am proud of myself for today:

1)

2)

3)

Something that calmed me down today was:

What I would like to say to my 'Anxious Self' today:

This is what I would like my grown up's to know today:

HEALTHY BODY: HEALTHY MIND

Helping my body stay healthy, also helps my mind:

Today I supported my body & mind by staying hydrated:

Water: Colour in the water bottles as you finish them

Getting enough sleep helps my brain face the day:

Tonight I will go to bed at: ____ pm

Date: ....

Today my anxiety level is: Low | Medium | High

I think that my anxiety today has been triggered by:

I plan to manage my anxiety today by using:

☐ Deep breathing   ☐ Grounding *(3 things)*

☐ Meditation   ☐ Aromatherapy

☐ Exercise   ☐ Talk Therapy

Three things I am proud of myself for today:

1)

2)

3)

Something that calmed me down today was:

What I would like to say to my 'Anxious Self' today:

This is what I would like my grown up's to know today:

HEALTHY BODY: HEALTHY MIND

Helping my body stay healthy, also helps my mind:

Today I supported my body & mind by staying hydrated:

Water: Colour in the water bottles as you finish them

Getting enough sleep helps my brain face the day:

Tonight I will go to bed at: ___ pm

Date: ....

Today my anxiety level is: Low | Medium | High

I think that my anxiety today has been triggered by:

I plan to manage my anxiety today by using:

☐ Deep breathing   ☐ Grounding *(3 things)*

☐ Meditation   ☐ Aromatherapy

☐ Exercise   ☐ Talk Therapy

Three things I am proud of myself for today:

1)

2)

3)

Something that calmed me down today was:

What I would like to say to my 'Anxious Self' today:

This is what I would like my grown up's to know today:

HEALTHY BODY: HEALTHY MIND

Helping my body stay healthy, also helps my mind:

Today I supported my body & mind by staying hydrated:

Water: Colour in the water bottles as you finish them

Getting enough sleep helps my brain face the day:

Tonight I will go to bed at: ____ pm

Date: ....

Today my anxiety level is: Low | Medium | High

I think that my anxiety today has been triggered by:

I plan to manage my anxiety today by using:

☐ Deep breathing   ☐ Grounding *(3 things)*

☐ Meditation   ☐ Aromatherapy

☐ Exercise   ☐ Talk Therapy

Three things I am proud of myself for today:

1)

2)

3)

Something that calmed me down today was:

What I would like to say to my 'Anxious Self' today:

This is what I would like my grown up's to know today:

HEALTHY BODY: HEALTHY MIND

Helping my body stay healthy, also helps my mind:

Today I supported my body & mind by staying hydrated:

Water: Colour in the water bottles as you finish them

Getting enough sleep helps my brain face the day:

Tonight I will go to bed at: _____ pm

Date: ....

Today my anxiety level is: Low | Medium | High

I think that my anxiety today has been triggered by:

I plan to manage my anxiety today by using:

☐ Deep breathing   ☐ Grounding *(3 things)*

☐ Meditation   ☐ Aromatherapy

☐ Exercise   ☐ Talk Therapy

Three things I am proud of myself for today:

1)

2)

3)

Something that calmed me down today was:

What I would like to say to my 'Anxious Self' today:

This is what I would like my grown up's to know today:

HEALTHY BODY: HEALTHY MIND

Helping my body stay healthy, also helps my mind:

Today I supported my body & mind by staying hydrated:

Water: Colour in the water bottles as you finish them

Getting enough sleep helps my brain face the day:

Tonight I will go to bed at: ____ pm

Date: ....

Today my anxiety level is: Low | Medium | High

I think that my anxiety today has been triggered by:

I plan to manage my anxiety today by using:

☐ Deep breathing ☐ Grounding *(3 things)*

☐ Meditation ☐ Aromatherapy

☐ Exercise ☐ Talk Therapy

Three things I am proud of myself for today:

1)

2)

3)

Something that calmed me down today was:

What I would like to say to my 'Anxious Self' today:

This is what I would like my grown up's to know today:

HEALTHY BODY: HEALTHY MIND

Helping my body stay healthy, also helps my mind:

Today I supported my body & mind by staying hydrated:

Water: Colour in the water bottles as you finish them

Getting enough sleep helps my brain face the day:

Tonight I will go to bed at: ___ pm

Date:

Today my anxiety level is: Low | Medium | High

I think that my anxiety today has been triggered by:

I plan to manage my anxiety today by using:

☐ Deep breathing   ☐ Grounding (3 things)

☐ Meditation   ☐ Aromatherapy

☐ Exercise   ☐ Talk Therapy

Three things I am proud of myself for today:

1)

2)

3)

Something that calmed me down today was:

What I would like to say to my 'Anxious Self' today:

This is what I would like my grown up's to know today:

HEALTHY BODY: HEALTHY MIND

Helping my body stay healthy, also helps my mind:

Today I supported my body & mind by staying hydrated:

Water: Colour in the water bottles as you finish them

Getting enough sleep helps my brain face the day:

Tonight I will go to bed at: ____ pm

Date: ....

Today my anxiety level is: Low | Medium | High

I think that my anxiety today has been triggered by:

I plan to manage my anxiety today by using:

☐ Deep breathing   ☐ Grounding *(3 things)*

☐ Meditation   ☐ Aromatherapy

☐ Exercise   ☐ Talk Therapy

Three things I am proud of myself for today:

1)

2)

3)

Something that calmed me down today was:

What I would like to say to my 'Anxious Self' today:

This is what I would like my grown up's to know today:

Helping my body stay healthy, also helps my mind:

Today I supported my body & mind by staying hydrated:

Water: Colour in the water bottles as you finish them

Getting enough sleep helps my brain face the day:

Tonight I will go to bed at: ____ pm

Date: ....

Today my anxiety level is: Low | Medium | High

I think that my anxiety today has been triggered by:

I plan to manage my anxiety today by using:

☐ Deep breathing   ☐ Grounding *(3 things)*

☐ Meditation   ☐ Aromatherapy

☐ Exercise   ☐ Talk Therapy

Three things I am proud of myself for today:

1)

2)

3)

Something that calmed me down today was:

What I would like to say to my 'Anxious Self' today:

This is what I would like my grown up's to know today:

HEALTHY BODY: HEALTHY MIND

Helping my body stay healthy, also helps my mind:

Today I supported my body & mind by staying hydrated:

Water: Colour in the water bottles as you finish them

Getting enough sleep helps my brain face the day:

Tonight I will go to bed at: ____ pm

Date: ....

Today my anxiety level is: Low | Medium | High

I think that my anxiety today has been triggered by:

I plan to manage my anxiety today by using:

☐ Deep breathing   ☐ Grounding *(3 things)*

☐ Meditation   ☐ Aromatherapy

☐ Exercise   ☐ Talk Therapy

Three things I am proud of myself for today:

1)

2)

3)

Something that calmed me down today was:

What I would like to say to my 'Anxious Self' today:

This is what I would like my grown up's to know today:

HEALTHY BODY: HEALTHY MIND

Helping my body stay healthy, also helps my mind:

Today I supported my body & mind by staying hydrated:

Water: Colour in the water bottles as you finish them

Getting enough sleep helps my brain face the day:

Tonight I will go to bed at: ___ pm

Date: ....

Today my anxiety level is: Low | Medium | High

I think that my anxiety today has been triggered by:

I plan to manage my anxiety today by using:

<table>
<tr><td>☐</td><td>Deep breathing</td><td>☐</td><td>Grounding (3 things)</td></tr>
<tr><td>☐</td><td>Meditation</td><td>☐</td><td>Aromatherapy</td></tr>
<tr><td>☐</td><td>Exercise</td><td>☐</td><td>Talk Therapy</td></tr>
</table>

Three things I am proud of myself for today:

1)

2)

3)

Something that calmed me down today was:

What I would like to say to my 'Anxious Self' today:

This is what I would like my grown up's to know today:

HEALTHY BODY: HEALTHY MIND

Helping my body stay healthy, also helps my mind:

Today I supported my body & mind by staying hydrated:

Water: Colour in the water bottles as you finish them

Getting enough sleep helps my brain face the day:

Tonight I will go to bed at: ___ pm

Date: ....

Today my anxiety level is: Low | Medium | High

I think that my anxiety today has been triggered by:

I plan to manage my anxiety today by using:

☐ Deep breathing ☐ Grounding *(3 things)*

☐ Meditation ☐ Aromatherapy

☐ Exercise ☐ Talk Therapy

Three things I am proud of myself for today:

1)

2)

3)

Something that calmed me down today was:

What I would like to say to my 'Anxious Self' today:

This is what I would like my grown up's to know today:

HEALTHY BODY: HEALTHY MIND

Helping my body stay healthy, also helps my mind:

Today I supported my body & mind by staying hydrated:

Water: Colour in the water bottles as you finish them

Getting enough sleep helps my brain face the day:

Tonight I will go to bed at: ____ pm

Printed in Great Britain
by Amazon